My First Book about the Alphabet of Mountain Animals

Amazing Animal Books Children's Picture Books

By Molly Davidson

Mendon Cottage Books

I0439618

JD-Biz Publishing

Read More Amazing Animal Books

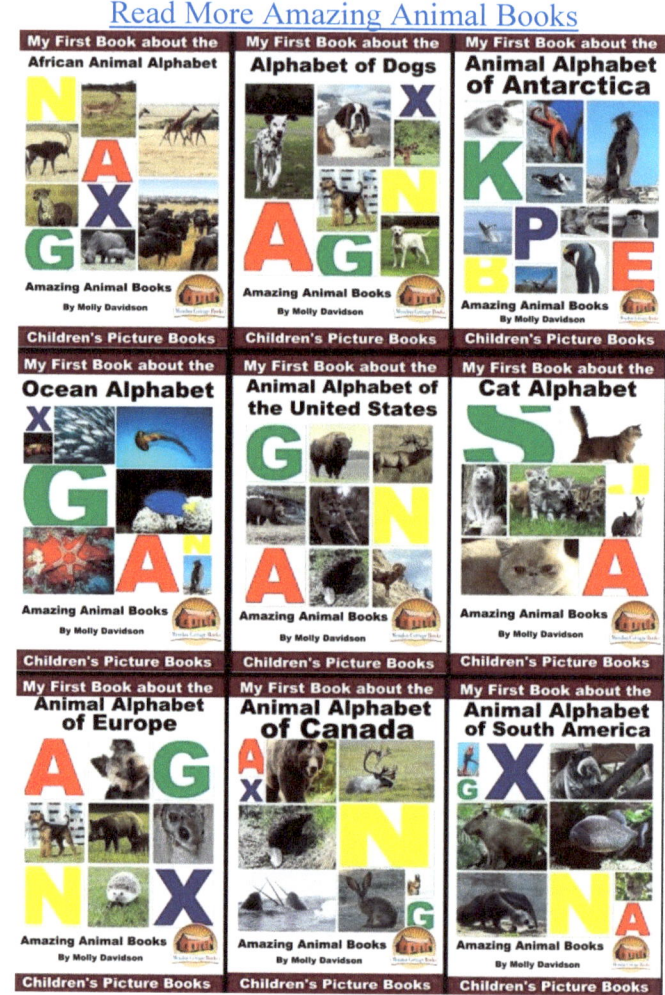

Purchase at Amazon.com

Download Free Books!
http://MendonCottageBooks.com

Introduction

About 20% of all land on Earth is mountains.

About 80 % of all the fresh water comes from the mountains.

Animals that live in the mountains have to be ready for little food, harsh winters, and uneven territory.

 **is for an Asiatic Black Bear.**

They live in the mountains of southern Asia.

Asiatic black bears eat mostly fruit and nuts from the various trees found in the tropical mountain forests.

They can run up to 25 mph (40 kph).

 **is for a Bison.**

Bison live mostly in the grassy meadows at the base of mountains in North America.

They are one of the largest types of cow, standing 6.5 ft (2 m) tall and weighing between 2,200 - 2,500 pounds (1,000 - 1,300 kg).

B is for also for a Big Horn Sheep.

Big horn sheep live in herds of 5 - 15 sheep in the Rocky Mountains of the U.S.

Their horns can be more than 30 inches across, and weigh up to 30 pounds!

Boys use their horns to fight for girls; some battles can last up to 24 hours.

C is for a Cougar.

Cougars are mostly found in the mountains of Canada and Mexico, but some live in Asia too.

They live to live alone and hunt deer, elk, and beaver.

D is for Deer.

Over 40 species of deer can be found living in herds of about 25, in Europe, Asia, and North America.

They can run about 43 mph (70 kph) and live between 10 - 20 years in the wild.

E is for an Eagle.

Eagles can be found living mostly in Asia, Europe, and North America.

Eagles can spot their prey from high in the air, and then they dive down as fast as 100 mph (160 kph) and snatch it up in their sharp talons.

E is also for an Echidna.

Echidna, also called spiky anteaters, live in the forests of Australia and New Guinea.

They have long tongues that they stick out to grab ants and termites.

 **is for a Fox.**

Fox scavenge for food mostly at night in forests and cities across the Northern hemisphere.

There are 12 different species of fox, but they all have long bushy tails which can easily be spotted as they run.

G
is for a Gorilla.

Gorillas live in groups of 5 - 30 in the mountain jungles of Africa.

They eat about 60 pounds (27 kg) of food per day, which includes berries, roots, leaves, and green vegetation.

 **is for a Himalayan Tahr.**

They live on the rocky mountain slopes of the Himalayas.

Himalayan tahrs are related to goats and eat mostly grass, leaves, and fruit.

I is for an Indochinese Tiger.

The Indochinese tiger is found in the mountain forests of south-east Asia, but they are almost extinct in the wild today.

They hunt by stalking their prey, then pounce upon it when it least expects.

They are able to run up to 60 mph (96 kph).

J is for a Japanese Macaque.

The Japanese Macaque is also called the snow monkey because it lives in the colder mountain regions of Japan.

 **is for a Klipspringer.**

Klipspringers, meaning rock jumpers, are small antelope that live on the rocky mountain cliffs in Africa.

They live in groups of two, and the boys have small straight horns.

L is for a Leopard.

Leopards live in Africa and Asia in the mountainous rainforests.

They hunt at night and spend most of the day up in a high tree in the shade.

About half of all leopards are solid black.

M is for a Moose.

Moose can be found in the cold mountains of North America and Europe.

They grow new antlers every spring; it takes them about 3 - 5 months to be fully grown.

 **is for a North American Beaver.**

The North American beaver can be found in lakes and streams in North American forests.

They are very good at building dams out of mud, twigs, and branches.

They can stay underwater for up to 15 minutes.

 **is for an Owl.**

Owls live in forests and mountains all over the World, except Antarctica.

They swallow their prey whole, and can eat up to 1,000 mice per year.

P is for a Ptarmigan.

Ptarmigan have been around since the Ice Age, living in the cold northern mountains of Canada, Europe, and Japan.

They have white feathers in the winter, which they molt off in the spring to brown feathers.

P is for also for a Panda.

Pandas live in the mountains of central and western China, where they are almost extinct.

They spend 12 - 15 hours per day eating bamboo; their main food source.

R is for a Reindeer.

Reindeer are also called caribou, and live in the North Mountains of Alaska, Canada, Russia, and Europe.

They have sharp tough hooves and foot pads, which help them, dig through the snow and ice to find food.

S **is for a Spectacled Bear.**

The spectacled bear, also called the Andean bear, lives in the Andes Mountains of South America.

T is for a Tapir.

Mountain tapir are found in the Andes Mountains of Colombia, Peru, and Ecuador.

They have a long, flexible nose that they use to eat leaves and branches.

They are great swimmers, and use water to help cool down.

U is for a Ursus Arctos, the scientific name for a Grizzly Bear.

They live in the mountains of North America.

Grizzly bears live close to streams and lakes, where they eat salmon and fish.

 **is for a Vicuna.**

Vicunas are cousins of camels and llamas, found in the Andes Mountains.

They live in herds of one boy and many girls.

They are the national animal of Peru.

 **is for a Wolf.**

Wolves have lived in mountains, for over 300,000 years, all over the World.

Wherever wolves live, they are the top predator, even killing other wolves.

They live about 10 years in the wild.

 **is for a Yellow-Bellied Marmot.**

A yellow - bellied marmot, also called a rock chuck, lives in the mountains of western Canada and the United States.

They live in a burrow as colonies (groups) of between 10 to 20 marmots.

Conclusion

I hope you have enjoyed reading about many different mountain animals.

One more fact: Most mountain animals migrate down the mountains in the winter and travel to the top in the summer, where it is cooler.

Download Free Books!

http://MendonCottageBooks.com

Purchase at Amazon.com
Website http://AmazingAnimalBooks.com

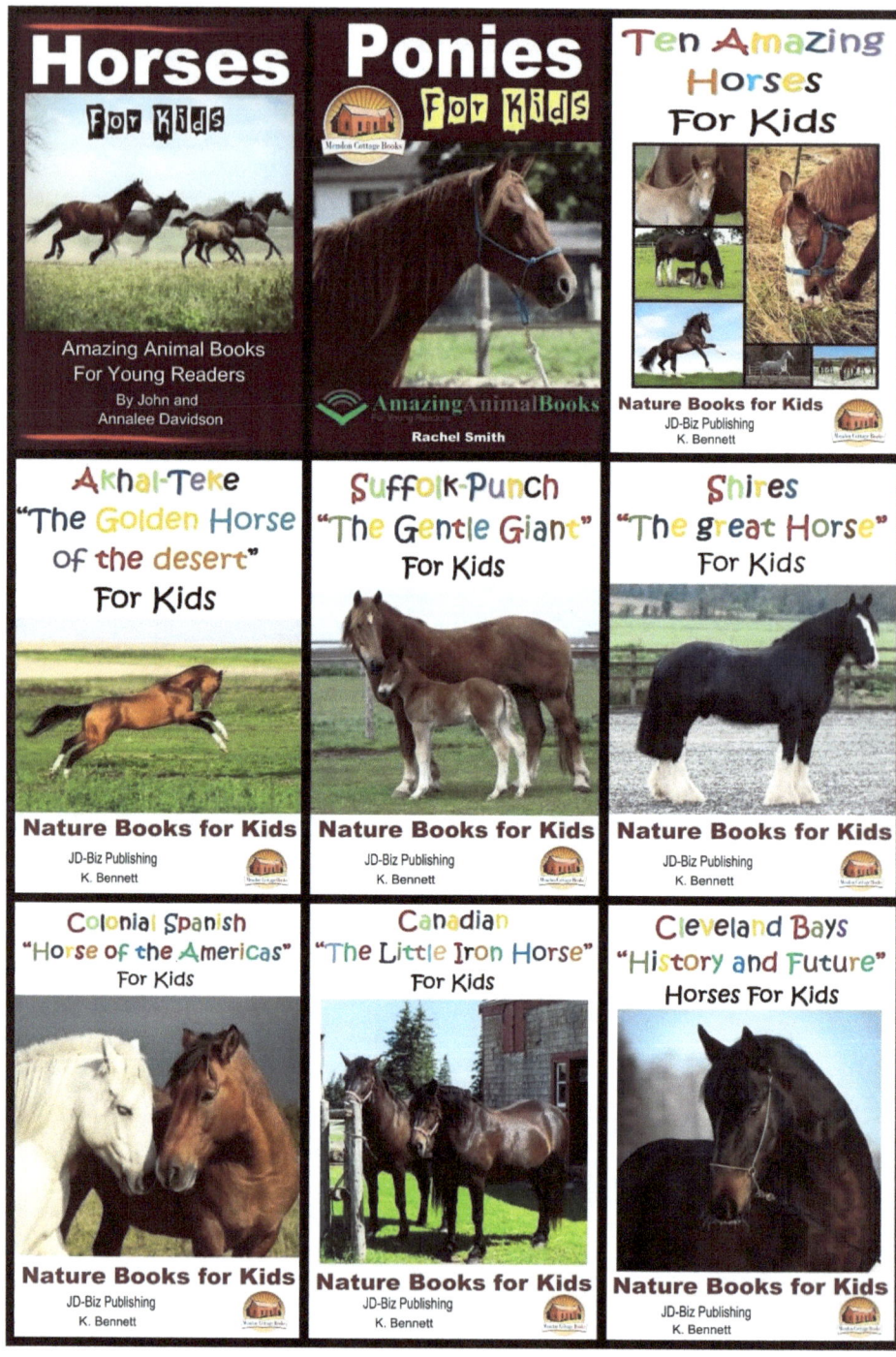

Our books are available at

1. Amazon.com

2. Barnes and Noble

3. Itunes

4. Kobo

5. Smashwords

6. Google Play Books

Download Free Books!
http://MendonCottageBooks.com

Publisher

JD-Biz Corp

P O Box 374

Mendon, Utah 84325

http://www.jd-biz.com/

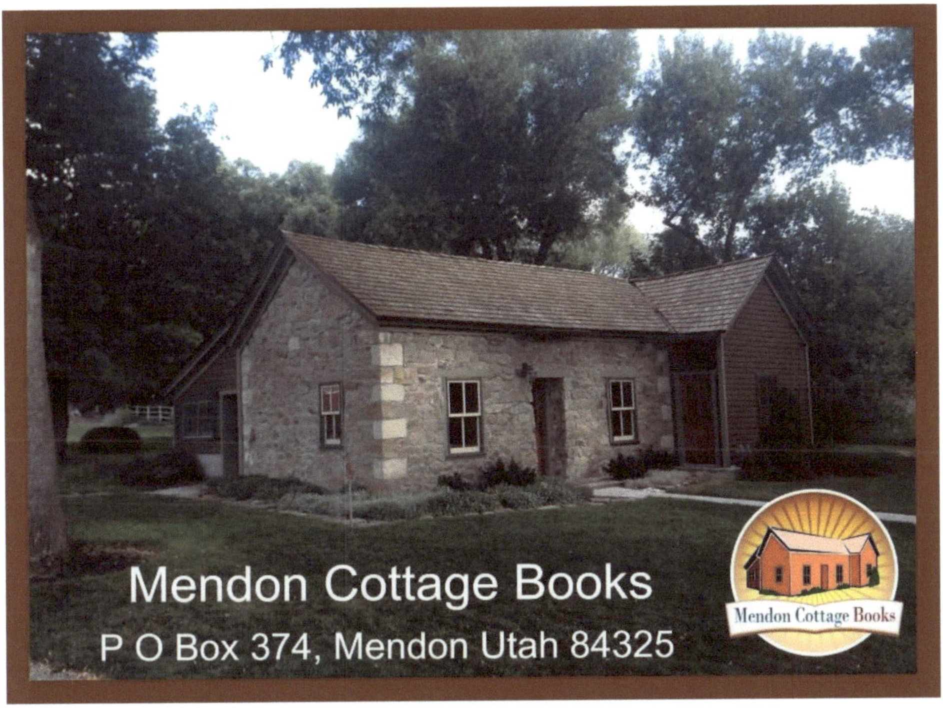

Mendon Cottage Books

P O Box 374, Mendon Utah 84325

www.ingramcontent.com/pod-product-compliance
Lightning Source LLC
Chambersburg PA
CBHW050902290526

45792CB00002B/675